COPYRIGHT NOTICE

51+ Networking Mistakes is protected by copyright law. The contents of this book may not be reproduced or transmitted in any form or by any means, electronic or mechanical, including photocopying, recording or by any information storage and retrieval system without written permission from the authors, except for the inclusion of brief quotations in a review.

© 2016-2026 by Bart Smith & Noa Schecter
ALL RIGHTS RESERVED WORLDWIDE
ISBN-13: 978-1539005148

For more information about *51+ Networking Mistakes*; individual orders; bundled orders, discounts for bulk-quantity purchases; audio products; interviews; information on seminars; JV opportunities; mentoring/consulting; booking one or both of the authors to speak at your next seminar, workshop or event; please contact the authors at their website or via LinkedIn:

NOA SCHECTER
EQEvolve.com
LinkedIn.com/in/NoaSchecter

BART SMITH
BartSmith.com
LinkedIn.com/in/BartSmith

ACKNOWLEDGMENTS

There are a number of people we'd like to thank for the inspiration to write this book. First, we'd like to acknowledge those who (in the past) conducted networking events where WE (the authors) learned a great number of mistakes on our own and what NOT to do the next time around. Thank you so much for all those experiences to be able to write a book like this. We'd also like to thank someone special for providing further inspiration to write this book. Having attended his networking events, and noticing the many mistakes being made, we gained further inspiration to write this book. Thank you so much for inviting us!

DEDICATIONS

This book is dedicated to everyone who loves to network, meet new people, grow their business or who just like to get out of the house every now and then. Oh, and for all those who say, "Whoops! That was a (networking) mistake I'll never repeat again ..." To all of you, a networking solute to you!

WHY WE WROTE THIS BOOK

To be honest? Because we had it in us to write another book! Noa wanted to write a second book, and I didn't cover enough about the "mistakes" people make when they network in my networking book called, My Networking Tactics. Hence, this book was born when the two of us were networking at an event together. We had witnessed mistake after mistake made by so many people at this event that it just inspired us to write this book! We hope you enjoy it and learn from it. We use it as our own guide for networking every time!

TABLE OF CONTENTS

As you can see, we essentially wrote this book in three main parts. The book is broken up into mistakes you should avoid **BEFORE**, **WHILE** and **AFTER** you go networking.

After reading this book and following as many of our suggestions as possible, see how your own networking **performance**, **results** and **success** improves rather INSTANTLY! Whenever you network, it's all about moving you forward with your goals and aspirations, whether personal and/or for your business.

PART I
AVOID THESE NETWORKING MISTAKES
BEFORE
YOU GO NETWORKING

PART II
AVOID THESE NETWORKING MISTAKES
WHILE
YOU ARE NETWORKING

PART III
AVOID THESE NETWORKING MISTAKES
AFTER
YOU GO NETWORKING

Bonus: *10* Social Media Networking Mistakes

MEET THE AUTHORS

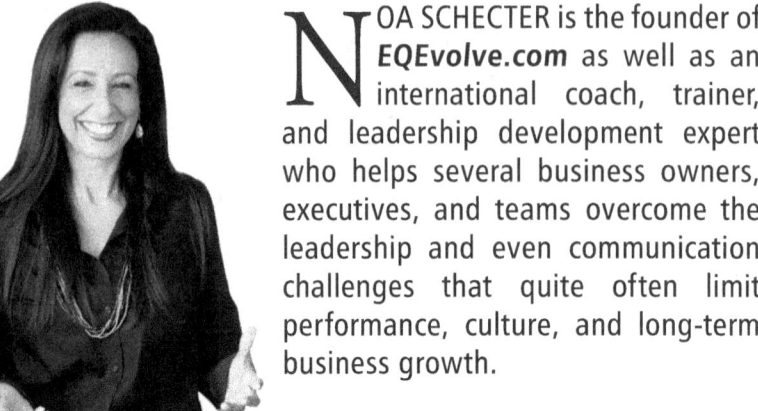

NOA SCHECTER is the founder of EQEvolve.com as well as an international coach, trainer, and leadership development expert who helps several business owners, executives, and teams overcome the leadership and even communication challenges that quite often limit performance, culture, and long-term business growth.

When communication is unclear, accountability is low, leadership is inconsistent, or team dynamics are not working, even great businesses struggle to grow. Noa helps leaders identify what is getting in the way and create practical strategies that strengthen leadership, improve

BART SMITH is the author of 35+ books on business, marketing, self-help, coaching, motivation, relationships, and, yes, ... NETWORKING! Check out Bart's books at his website, **BartSmith.com**. You'll be amazed at the variety of topics written about to enhance your life.

One of Bart's passions (and businesses) is baking the world's best chocolate chip cookies since 1988. Really, check out and order some at: **BartsCookies.com!!!**

PART 1

AVOID THESE NETWORKING MISTAKES

BEFORE
YOU GO
NETWORKING

REMIND YOURSELF "WHY" YOU'RE NETWORKING IN THE FIRST PLACE

Get amped, jacked up, excited to network. If you're like everyone else out there, you're going out to network for some of the following reasons:

1. **To find PEOPLE YOU CAN HELP** with your product/service or with a referral. We can't help everyone, personally, but we can if we have our own group of people who we can refer you to for services.

2. **To find PEOPLE WHO CAN HELP YOU** with your needs. If need resources, ask, "Do you know anyone who can _____? I'm looking for someone who can _____."

3. **To make NEW FRIENDS and more.** You never know when meeting someone could turn into a new friendship, party/event invite, or something more meaningful even a _____! DATING/MARRIAGE! Hey, dating and marriage usually starts with two people meeting one another at some kind of event, right? That's called networking with the ultimate return ... a life mate! Now, if you're already married or not interested in dating, then networking is still a great opportunity for meeting new people.

PREPARE FOR THE EVENT

DO NOT WASTE YOUR TIME walking into an event unprepared. Whether your goal is personal or business, plan ahead. Know the event that you are attending. Create a preparation CHECKLIST customized for your needs. On that list, you might expand upon such topics.

RESEARCH THE EVENT, ORGANIZATION AND/OR PEOPLE ASSOCIATED WITH THE NETWORKING EVENT BEFORE YOU ATTEND

Where are you going tonight? What's the main theme for this event? Who's hosting it? What's the company about that's sponsoring the event? These are great questions you'll want answers for.

Get to know the answers to these questions PRIOR to attending the event. Don't walk in and ask, "So, what's this all about? Who's putting this event on?" Be informed. Visit the website, eMail the host, do a little research. You know the drill. At a minimum, take 5-10 minutes and do this. It'll pay off when you walk through the door excited to greet the host with a, "Hi, I read about this online and thought it was a great event to attend." By researching the event, you might also learn what the dress code is, what kind of location/building/place you're going to, where to park, local restaurants, etc. so you know what you can expect.

WHAT IS YOUR OUTCOME? DO YOU HAVE ONE?

Know what your expectations are. What do you want to get out of networking? Before you go to any type of an event, go with intention and not because you have nothing better to do, per se. Killing time is not going to help you move forward in life. What's more, others are going to think you're not really interested in being there. Time is precious for all of us. Value your time (and others'). If you live near a big city where there are hundreds/thousands of events taking place, be selective. While your options are endless, time for networking with the right people to generate interest in your product or business, choose wisely. So, before you go to a workshop or event, think hard about what your goals are for the event so you can maximize your presence there. Why is a particular event important to you?

Network with Bart Smith at his website → **BartSmith.com**

PART 1 – BEFORE YOU GO NETWORKING

- You might go to a certain event because there is a certain person there you want to meet. Don't waste anyone's time.

- Maybe there are people there who can add value to your business. For example, if you're in real estate or you're looking for investors, you might go golfing with a group of people. Specifically, go to place where people have the capacity to advance your goals.

- If you're single and you're looking to introduce yourself to other single people, then you are going to go to an event that has to do with single people.

- Target your efforts to a target market for whatever your needs are.

- If you're promoting a product, it is good to go out and practice your pitch on others, share your success stories, learn what you should do/say and shouldn't and then, branch out to the next event sharper and wiser than the last one; better prepared to meet new people whom you can introduce what it is that you do with greater precision and impact.

- Before you go to an event, write down a small list of concrete, tangible goals: At least, have them in mind before you venture out.

"I am going to meet x-amount of people, and plan to come away with y-number of sales/leads."

"When I go home, I want to have an x-amount of business cards, or have introduced x-number of people to my product/service."

Write out what you wish to get out of the event before you leave the house. Having your own personalized list of goals for why networking is important to you and what you want out of it will help manifest the exact results you want for all your efforts when attending. What's more, have a goal for every event you go to. Be clear about your intentions and know the motivation behind attending the event.

With all that in mind, try attending at least one networking event once a week if possible. If you go two or three times a week, that's even better. Again, just don't go to make an appearance. Make an IMPACT by making sure the event is really for you. Be clear why you are attending the event, what you plan to get out of it (i.e., new clients, leads, sales, a date, new friends, new career ideas, a few new business cards, etc.).

GOING TO THE EVENT
TO BE ON TIME ... OR NOT!

For starters, you do want to be on time when you can, especially if this is your first time for many reasons. Do not miss any introductory speeches or the chance to meet everyone as they go around a circle introducing one another. If you're late, you might miss the opportunity to get to know a number of people, quickly, giving you the chance to note, *"Oh, I want to talk to that person and that person over there, too."*

Another reason to get there early is to get comfortable with the environment, especially is you're shy. Getting there early will provide you with enough time to warm up and introduce yourself to others so that by the time the room fills up you will feel like you already know most people.

Some events, as we stated, have lectures at the beginning or some kind of group exercise. You can imagine how awkward you (or others) might feel if they walk into the room late when people are already engaged in an exercise or activity.

By getting to the event on time, you're in a good position to help others connect with others, which should always be one of your goals. Ultimately, you end up meeting everyone by introducing others to the group. Indirectly, you'll be better able to scope out people, what they do, how you might work with them (or not) without putting yourself in a situation that MIGHT be uncomfortable. REMEMBER, you become somebody instantly when everyone is talking about how you helped others in the room by asking good questions such as how their business is, their profession, career, hobby or passion.

On the other hand, being late can have its advantages, too. While everyone is busy and distracted meeting and greeting, you can scope out the room to see who's talking to whom and you get a feel for the event by asking people, *"So, how's the event going for you? What have I missed? Fill me in ..."*

Also, if the event did turn out to be not what you expected, you didn't waste too much time there, and you can quickly leave. What's more, by you making a late entrance, people might turn to see who's walking in the door. Oh, YOU! What a way to make a grand entrance, right? Smile, get situated and when it comes time to networking ... get right to it!

LOOK YOUR BEST, ALWAYS

Even though you've been told that the dress code for the event is business casual, NEVER dress down, dress UP! Look sharp, yet comfortably groomed, and dressed appropriately for the event. It seems obvious, but let's remind ourselves, GUYS: Clean shaven (or well groomed), smelling good, looking good, walking tall, and ready to meet the crowd. LADIES: Professionally dressed, well organized, looking your best, and smiling from start to finish.

For those on a tight budget, you can shop at any number of outlet stores in your area; even if you have to drive to one. Make a special trip and shop 'til you drop to ensure you have the right clothing. Be sure to have a few basic outfits, such as (GUYS) black slacks and an assortment of different shirts. Don't wear the same three outfits time after time. In today's world. Sometimes, it's okay to show up wearing jeans and a nice button down shirt. Cool sneakers are all right, unless you know for sure that the dress code is formal. For example, the dress code anywhere near the beach is usually less formal than if you were to go to an event in the heart of the city.

While shopping, you can buy name brand shirts on sale/clearance. You'd be quite surprised to find many items are about 90% less than the original retail price at some of the outlet stores. Be patient, shop around, shop often to get a sense of style and save up! Shop for yourself at least once a quarter, if not every other month provided you can afford it. You might also buy clothes for specific networking events to make a lasting impression. Over time, build your wardrobe gradually, but do build it! Also, second hand stores and some nonprofit organizations help people dress people for an interview. Check out *Dress for Success: Worldwide*.

Also, you might ask the dry cleaners to box your clothes keep things nice/neat. If you need to wear a button down shirt that needs to be ironed, and you're going to keep it in the car (or if you travel), always ask the cleaners to box the clothes. Ask for starch so that they won't wrinkle easily. It's better to have a gym bag in the car for extra clothing, extra toiletries, socks (two pair, maybe). You may be at work and you hear about a networking opportunity. When you're prepared, you won't be left out and you won't miss an opportunity because you are unprepared.

If you are on a tight budget, you can always go to a clothing outlet or discount stores where you'll find great deals on very inexpensive items. As long as you buy the basics, it will not cost you much. It is recommended that you keep two outfits in your car. One is professional and for casual wear. You never know when you'll be asked to a networking event.

MAKE AN AMAZING FIRST IMPRESSION WITH EVERYONE

How's your energy? You know, how's that fire inside you that's burning to meet knew people and to share what you do while helping others at the same time? Having the right energy when you walk into a room or reach out to shake someone's hand is everything when making that first grand impression.

MAKE EVERY FIRST ENCOUNTER COUNT!

What if you don't feel like networking? What if you don't feel like going out to network? Have you ever noticed that when you had to go to an event that you didn't feel like attending or you had an opinion about, or maybe you were just tired, that in the end it was a complete waste of your time. We've all been there. You show up to the event and by the end of the night you find yourself saying to yourself: *"Self, I was right about this and should have stayed home!"* That being said, for the future, our advice to you is ... stay home! Why? Because, if that's the way you feel before the event, chances are, you might also feel that way or worse during the event thinking you'd rather be somewhere else. That's no impression to leave with people you meet.

We've all been to events that bored us or were unsuccessful in teaching us something new (or benefit from). What did in each case though was to show up with the right mindset/attitude and had an amazing time. No matter how bad the event itself might be, there is always usually great people to meet, new friends to make and even new business ideas and partners to entertain.

We've also been to events where we spent much of our time in the hotel lobby, bar, restaurant, coffee shop, or parking lot talking until all hours of the night because of the awesome experience. If you think about it, while you read this book, we can attest that 80% of the people we know in our own business contacted us through networking. That says a lot about what you can expect from networking and the kind of exciting and enthusiastic people we meet and you will meet too if you get out and network.

WHAT TO DO & BRING TO AN EVENT
MARKETING MATERIALS

If you have something to sell, don't just tell people about it, give them samples to take home with them. Go to your event with a postcard, flyer, handout, brochure, tri-fold, anything that tells people what you do so you don't have to explain every detail about your business. Have you written a book or two? Do you have a YouTube channel primed with videos? Create a handout that looks like a menu showcasing all your books and/or videos. Let people visually see what you do and let them ask questions that interests them instead of you monopolizing a conversation. Most people will either tune out or forget what you said anyway, because they have several other people to talk to besides you

By you giving them something for them to take home, you'll be remembered and your contact information is readily available. So, keep extra marketing materials with you in your car, or better yet, keep digital copies of them on your phone.

Network with Bart Smith at his website → **BartSmith.com**

PART 1 – BEFORE YOU GO NETWORKING

We've been to some events where people don't have business cards or they run out during the evening. It happens. Just be prepared. While we're on the subject of business cards, yes there are some companies that offer free, cheaply made business cards. Choose wisely and opt to pay an additional $5-15 to have them printed on quality card stock. The point is, you want to make a good impression. Another good idea is to have business cards people can write on, such as the back. You might go with a glossy front covering and a matte finish on the back, which makes it easy to make notes.

If someone is interested, simply get their eMail or phone number and send it to them (via eMail or text attachment). Done! This is actually a great way to save money on business cards. Make a digital one, keep it in your phone, and when someone asks you for your card, you can say you're all out, but, you'll send them a digital one. It has all the information. You could even take a hi-res picture of your current business card for use with this idea. There's no need to design something new; take a picture of what you currently have.

For those you who have multiple events coming up, whether you're attending or conducting them, and you use marketing materials to announce your upcoming events, we like to create small postcards and/or flyers or handouts with a blank space or an area designated for the date and location. We'll then print labels to type the event time, date and location, which you can affix to those handouts. We might also list all our services, pricing, testimonials, and website(s) (for more information), etc. Naturally, as you hand out these materials, in exchange, get their business cards (or information) so you can follow up. Be sure to ask if they have any questions, etc. Always keep the momentum going! We actually talk more about this in PART 3: AFTER THE NETWORKING EVENT. You guessed it ... FOLLOW-UP!

Network with Noa Schecter at her website → **EQevolve.com**

PREPARE TO BUILD YOUR (EMAIL) LIST WHILE YOU'RE AT THE NETWORKING EVENT

Take clipboards with three columns on it, one for eMail, name, and telephone number (in case you can't read their handwriting) to a networking event. As you circulate and tell people what you do, you can ask them if they'd like to join your eMail list right there on the spot. You can mention that by signing up, for a promotion, they might receive something free. (i.e., book excerpts, free report, free audio/video eCourse, etc.) As one person in your circle is filling in their name and information, others will observe and generally chime in. If you do this at every event, you might be able to grow your list by 10-30 people. Networking just 3 times a month can generate 90+ people who might join your list. Not bad!

PREPARE TO BRING COUPONS, SPECIAL OFFERS & OTHER ITEMS TO GIVE AWAY

Everybody wants to be a winner! You don't have to be conducting the event to invite people to join in on some fun with you. AT your event, you might offer a free book or something in exchange for people's name and eMail address. You can pick the winner at the event or when you get home. It's a great way to follow up with people. "Hey, you won one of my _____." Or, "You were one of the lucky 10 people who won one of my _____."

BE PREPARED TO SELL YOUR BOOKS/PRODUCT & ACCEPT MONIES ON THE SPOT

If you have a tangible product to sell, or even if you have a service, don't show up without the subtle intentions of selling something. You just never know. Make sure that you have a sample on hand, even if you keep it in the car. When you scope out the scene, you can always say, "*I have some product in the car. Let me run and get some to show you ...*" Don't hesitate to carry product with you. People respond better to visuals versus having to read marketing materials.

If you are unable to provide samples of your products or services, don't miss the opportunity to get their information. You can send them samples later via eMail/mail when you get back to your office or at least more information based on their interest and their questions. Remember, don't sound scripted like a tele-marketer. Definitely have an overall idea or plan for what you're going to say, highlighting the major points, but also allowing the conversation flow.

Bottom line, don't show up without the means to sell product (i.e., order forms, credit card readers/apps).

ADD YOUR PHOTO TO YOUR BUSINESS CARDS & OTHER MARKETING MATERIALS

If this means getting NEW business cards because your current business cards don't have your photo on them, yes, by all means consider doing so. We all know this is true ... Count how many business cards you took home without pictures on them. Can you describe what each person looked life? You can't. Be different and have your photo on your business card or other marketing material to stand out above all others. Be sure your photo is on everything you distribute at networking events. If are unable to do this, then eMail information with a photo of yourself, ideally a head shot of yourself. With your photo, they'll remember that you were the one helping others to acclimate and the conversation you both had. Oh, and that really great outfit or suit/shirt you bought for the event really enhanced your photo. That was a great investment.

Network with Noa Schecter at her website → **EQevolve.com**

BRING CASH NOT JUST A CREDIT CARD

You never know when you'll see something you want to buy (like a book or other product) or something to eat or drink. About $20-40 should do it. Some events you attend might not offer any (complimentary) food or drink you like. If you get hungry or thirsty, the bar might only take cash. For some, it's hard to network when you're hungry or thirsty. You might also want to treat someone to a drink or lunch/dinner that you're interested in networking with.

Another reason for cash is PARKING! Some parking structures only take cash. It's rare, but do keep it in mind. One more reason to bring cash is for tipping. Valet drivers, bartenders, servers, anyone who gives you a helping hand has earned a tip. Keep cash on hand for them. There are some places that only take cash and unless you know it, be prepared.

Some people aren't big on carrying cash, as credit cards show an easy record for all transactions for tax purposes. Keeping receipts for cash (even asking for them) can be a chore to manage. Nonetheless, take out $100 cash and make it last for six months. Hopefully, you won't go out networking every night of the week. But, you get the idea.

Keep the cash in an envelope and take it with you. When you need cash, you've got it. Otherwise, return it to your desk to be used again when you head to your next networking event. Treat it like your own little networking piggy bank. Withdraw as needed.

REHEARSE WHAT YOU WILL SAY

Don't show up tongue tied! This is a networking event! Have a few lines rehearsed and ready to share. Here are 5 key questions you'll ask everyone you meet. Need more ideas? Check out Bart's book, MY NETWORKING TACTICS for dozens of conversation starters and some for "exiting" a conversation when you know you want out of a conversation.

The best thing you can ever do in a conversation is to ask questions! Continue asking, even turning the conversation back around to the other person. As you keep the other person engaged, he/she keeps feeding you information about how you might be able to help them (or not). You certainly don't need to keep hearing yourself tell your own story again and again from one person to the next. Instead, ask questions throughout the event, comment, ask another, comment and then when the other person's dying to hear what you do, you can lay it on them in bite-sized, understandable nuggets, of course. Keep them wanting more. Never leave them fully satisfied so craft your responses in such a way to keep people interested, *"Wow, that's fascinating. I'm so glad we met. Can I get your card?"* Then, you say. *"I don't have one, but if you give me yours I'll text/email you my information today!"*

AVOID THESE "PERSONAL" NETWORKING MISTAKES

DRESS UP FOR THE EVENT

One thing we always insist with our clients (and ourselves) is that we dress our best for every networking event. You'd be surprised at how some people dress when they meet new strangers (i.e., potential clients, partners, investors, etc.) for the first time. Remember, this is a professional networking event, not a dinner party over at a friend's house. You'd think some people just woke up, maybe they thought it'd be okay to dress for a relaxed and comfortable casual hip feel, or maybe they hadn't shopped for a new outfit (deserving as they are for an event like this) in years and they picked out something tired and worn to represent themselves. Yikes! Not that this might apply to you, but don't let your guard down. Dress up, dress your best, dress to impress and remember, you're going to be in photos! Need ideas? You can look at fashion magazines (even for a quick second on the shelf) to see what's in or out of style. You can also look to see what store mannequins are showcasing and get ideas. You can also get ideas from people you see at the events you go to. If you really like his/her style, compliment the person and ask about the outfit. When someone dresses in a way that it is out of your budget, you can always buy something similar from cost effective stores.

Check what kind of event you're attending and even check with the host when possible. *"What's the dress code for the event?"* Whatever it is, step it up a notch. Remember, you're going to be in pictures or on video! So, look your best! If you are not sure, send an eMail and ask. Now, if your attire represents who you are, what you do, the industry you're in, by all means, dress for to give the right impression. If you're presenting or the host, there's no exception. You have to dress like a professional. We were at an event where the host was dressed in loose jeans (almost falling down), a large short sleeved, unbuttoned shirt and old tennis shoes. Seriously, you' never would have known this guy was the host. Dress the part you're supposed to be/play so people will instantly know who you are or what you're there to do.

In another quick example, we heard a story where a friend of ours was asked to present his services to a group of financial advisors. Well, he showed up without a tie. Fortunately, the bellboy at the hotel loaned him his tie so he could make the presentation. This was all done last minute, which brings us to this great tip to keep in mind before any networking event.

Network with Bart Smith at his website → **BartSmith.com**

BRING EXTRA CLOTHING

Keep extra sets of clothing in your car in case you feel the need to change, refresh yourself, or other reason. Maybe you just want to change out of your wrinkled, day's end clothing into something fresher, more comfortable (or dressy), but keep it professional. Keep a gym bag or even a carry on in the car with any and all accessories. For women, that means extra shoes (that are more comfortable for standing and walking around for a few hours) for the event or other purpose. For guys, that means fresh shirts, clean slacks, new or clean socks, an extra pair of shoes. Travel with 2-3 extra wardrobe changes if needed. You'll be glad you did when you walk through those networking event doors.

CHECK YOURSELF OUT ... REALLY, DO IT!
(BEFORE YOU ENTER ANY EVENT / ROOM)

"Do I look good, hot, handsome/beautiful, or what! All right, let's go!" That's what you should be able to say to yourself upon entering any room filled with potential strangers, clients, prospects, new found friends, etc. So, before you enter a room filled with total strangers, take a quick minute and head to the rest room to check yourself out. Up and down, front and back. Check your teeth (for food particles). If you don't have a mirror handy, a bathroom, even a cell phone can capture your image Some cell phones have a mirror so pretend you are taking a selfie. This way you can check yourself again. Check for stains on your clothing, wash your hands/face, straighten out that loose tie, tuck in that shirt, pull up those pants, ... you get the idea.

Straighten up and fly right into that room like an F14 jet flying over the crowd to make that first WOW impression! People are watching! If there isn't a rest room, then take a quick look in any mirror or building/car window, etc. Just don't walk into a room to network without checking yourself out first ... We want you to look good, great, hot, handsome/beautiful!

"SNIFF, SNIFF! HOW DO YOU ... SMELL?"

Seriously. That goes for our breath and body odor. We can't always tell if we have bad breath, but one thing's for sure, we can always carry with us some gum or mints. Pop a few into your mouth before you go into a room to meet new people. Carry a toothbrush and Tooth Soap to brush your teeth, tongue and gums. Seriously. You know how offensive it can be otherwise.

For the guys, body odor is a biggy and a no-no! After a long day, it's easy to not smell so fresh. So? You might want to have on hand, or in your car, deodorant, aftershave, cologne and mouthwash, especially if your are coming from work or the gym. Have a small travel bag (for both guys and gals) containing hand wipes, tissues, hand sanitizer, toothbrush, aspirin, even a small first aid kit with Band-Aids, Neosporin, etc.

This makes sense, right? We all think we don't need to tend to matters like this. We assume everything will be all right. The problem is, you just never know when you might need these things. Prepare once so you never have to be caught off guard if/when the moment comes when you smell, you have a stain on your shirt, you had garlic for lunch ... you name it!

CLEAN YOUR CAR

This is a must before the event. You don't want to be the one chosen to drive everyone down the street to a great restaurant when your car is a MESS! No one likes to ride around in a junk yard on wheels especially if you are trying to impress potential clients, investors or the opposite sex for a potential dating opportunity. If you have a decent size trunk, buy 1-2 inexpensive plastic boxes from Office Depot or a container store and put all of your books, papers, and anything else in there. Get everything out of the cab of your car and into the trunk.

You also might find/use a multi-purpose gym bag for staying overnight at a friend's house should there be a last minute decision. You might be traveling a great distance to an event and get an invitation such as, "*Why don't you just crash at my place, and we'll go to the event. Tomorrow we can have breakfast and you can return to your place.*" Should you work in an area that requires you to take public transportation, you could have such a box and/or bag like this at your office for just the right occasion. DON'T BE CAUGHT OFF GUARD ... PLAN/PREPARE!

LADIES, NO MESSY PURSES

Ladies, if your purse is a mess, don't open it! Make sure to place your pen and business card where it's easy to find/access without going into your unkept purse where you can never find anything.

BEFORE YOU NETWORK "CHECKLIST"

Were you able to create a workable checklist BEFORE you went networking? Was it pretty much on target? Well, to help keep you organized, on track and in line with our recommendations, here's a quick checklist you might use every time you go networking. Review and check off what applies and customize or add to this list as you see fit.

Network with Noa Schecter at her website → **EQevolve.com**

PREPARE FOR THE EVENT

- ❏ Remind yourself "why" you're networking in the first place (i.e., customers, clients, leads, investors, new friends, new career ideas, socializing, dating, etc.).
- ❏ What is your outcome? Do you have one?
- ❏ What are your goals for the event?
- ❏ Dress for success, dress up, and dress to kill.
- ❏ Rehearse what you will say. What are your best lines, elevator speech, statements to start and exit a conversation?
- ❏ Bring cash, not just a credit card, to the event.
- ❏ Prepare a means to accept monies if you happen to sell something at the event. If you happen to have your books (or other products with you) and someone asks, "How much is that?" They're asking because they want to buy it right then and there. Be prepared with mobile payment methods, cash on hand for change, etc.
- ❏ What's the parking like where you're going? Read the signs and don't park where NO parking allowed, etc

WHAT TO BRING TO AN EVENT

- ❏ Marketing materials (i.e., postcard, flyers, press releases, handouts, brochures, tri-folds, anything that tells people what you do so you don't have to go into lengthy explanations.
- ❏ Means to collect money from sales you might make when people ask you, "How much is this?" Bring order forms, mobile apps for accepting payments, $50-100 cash for change. (i.e., $20's, $10's, $5's, $1's, etc.)

Network with Bart Smith at his website → **BartSmith.com**

PART 1 – BEFORE YOU GO NETWORKING

- ❑ Clipboard with name, eMail and phone number columns. Another column you might add would be OCCUPATION. Bringing this is so you can build your eMail list.
- ❑ Add your photo on your business cards or other marketing materials
- ❑ Check what kind of event you're attending. Do a little homework in case you want to bring something special to a particular event.
- ❑ Bring extra clothing; keep it in the car, etc.
- ❑ Check yourself out (before you enter any event / room). Make sure you look your best.
- ❑ Sniff, sniff! How do you smell?
- ❑ Clean your car. No junk yards on wheels.
- ❑ Ladies, no messy purses.

GOING TO THE EVENT

- ❑ Be on time (or not for all the right reasons)
- ❑ Check your energy? Are you pumped, amped, and ready to shine like the sun when you walk in? All eyes are on you, remember! You're a star networker.
- ❑ Make every first encounter count!

What else can you think of? Make note of it and make it happen.

Now, let's talk about what kinds of mistakes you should watch out for WHILE attending a networking event!

PART 2

AVOID THESE NETWORKING MISTAKES

WHILE
YOU ARE NETWORKING

WHAT'S YOUR MAIN PURPOSE FOR BEING THERE?

"IT AIN'T ABOUT YOU! IT'S ABOUT THEM!"

You may get a little nervous and overanxious before any networking event. After all, you're about to meet a huge group of total strangers for the first time! For many people, they have a number of questions running through their mind before such an event, such as ...

> *Who will I meet? What will I say? Will they like me? Will I like them? Will I find the help I need? Will I find any business there for me? Can I be of any assistance to others and possibly get paid for it?*

With all those great questions and concerns, there's one important question that will answer all of your questions?

Every time we go networking, we think about one thing in particular ...

"How can I help the people I meet?"

That one question sets everything else on the right course to bring ensure things go your way and in your favor ...

Network with Noa Schecter at her website → **EQevolve.com**

- **Will they like me?** WHO DOESN'T like someone who offers to help them. You will have instant fans from folks who you offer to help ... "*Will I find people who can help me?*" Who doesn't find people who can help them when you make an effort to be of service to them first? You know the old saying, "*Help others get what they want, and they'll help you get what you want.*"

- **Will I meet anyone I like there?** By focusing on the other person's needs more (80/20 rule), you get a front row seat into listening to everything the other person has to offer. By the end of that 5-10 minute conversation, you know everything you need to know to make a snap decision whether to go forward with the person or not. This is something you can't do if you're doing most of the talking.

- **Will this event be worth my time?** You'll know with confidence if the event was worth it by how you turned everyone around to what you have to offer, which you did when you focused on others first. By asking questions, listening, cultivating more interest, filtering answers you receive from different people ... it'll be natural for you to deduce, "*Wow, this event turned out great! I scored a lot of new acquaintances, made some new friends, found a few new clients, got some great ideas for my own business, ...*" Remember it is not about how many business cards you collect or the number of people in the room; it's about the quality of your leads that are generated from the event.

To summarize the first mistake most people make -- People tend to talk too much about themselves or the way they present themselves isn't structured, rehearsed, or prepared so they speak in random sentences, which is more reason why you need to take control of the conversation. You know what to do. Extract information from other people to find out if you can help them and ultimately they may be able to help you. Even if we can't help

Network with Bart Smith at his website → BartSmith.com

someone, just by listening and showing genuine interest, you might make a new friend who would love to refer you to people he/she knows who may be inspired to hear what you have to say and potentially buy what you are selling right there on the spot!

Noa, has a good friend who always starts off his networking meetings by saying to everyone, "Be of service first. *Ask people how you can help or support them.*" We take that same approach to the maximum! The results? It's always a win-win situation for everyone. Who doesn't want that?

DON'T WAIT TO BUILD YOUR NETWORK. BUILD IT NOW SO IT'S IN PLACE WHEN YOU NEED IT!

Today is not soon enough to start building your network when you need a group of people to rely on for referrals, repeat business, business ideas and/or recommendations on services and products to help you with your business. Don't wait to build your network until you need it. Start now, manage it, and keep your contacts fresh and growing.

Get into the habit of calling people you haven't heard from in awhile to maintain those contacts. Today, with Facebook and social media, it's even easier for you to follow up with your friends and colleagues online and send a nice message to them periodically. Sending eCards to wish people a happy birthday, or even sending a card that requires a stamp can make a good impression. It means that you took time to write a note and you value the relationship. Maintain an up-to-date database of contacts and stay in touch.

BRING YOUR OWN NAME TAG

Most networking events rarely supply name tags. You pay at the door (or online), show up, walk in and start meeting and greeting while introducing and reintroducing yourself to people.

Network with Noa Schecter at her website → **EQevolve.com**

TIP: Create your own name tag with your website address on it or a photo of your product or one of your book covers, etc. TIP: If name tags aren't supplied, have your own to make it easy for people to know your name in seconds. You being the only person with a name tag also sets you apart from the rest of the crowd. Did you attend a networking event in the past where they gave you a really cool looking name tag? Keep it for your next event otherwise make your own and slip it into the casing from your last event.

If you do make your own, make a few, and always take them to events. Also be sure to include your title and website address on it. Remember, this is a custom job so your design is your own, but keep it simple and informative. Now, what if you have a name tag from another event and they have their event credential on it? If you like it, use the idea to create your own.

DISCONNECT FROM TECH

Disconnect from your electronics so you can be 100% present. How many people do you see at networking events texting or checking their phone for voice messages and eMail? Virtually, everyone wrapped around a mobile device is not engaged in networking. Don't YOU be that kind of person with your head buried in your phone when it should be up, looking around and eager to meet other networkers.

Someone who is looking to meet you doesn't want to see that you're too busy even though you're just doodling on your phone to kill time. Talk about lost opportunity. You can check all those eMails and text messages when you are on a break away from the crowd or departing. Put your phone in your pocket, purse or briefcase and leave it there. Got a family? Sure, check it if it vibrates, otherwise, you don't need it to network. Who hasn't used their phone as an excuse to leave an event or meeting prematurely.

If you did your homework, you should be at an event that is going to be worth the time you put into it. So, unless it's an emergency, networking is not a place for phones with few exceptions.

BRANDING IS EVERYTHING, AND YOUR BRAND IS YOU! SO, PROMOTE IT, BUILD IT, PUBLICIZE IT!

Depending on what you do, YOU are the BRAND people need to meet, so know and engage with your products and services. Do this proudly and confidently by being of service to others in what you do and how you do it.

> "Wow, Bart / Noa is really great to talk to. They were so into what I was doing and offered a number of innovative ideas for me on promoting my business. That meant a lot to me. I'm going to call them after the event to arrange a time when we can get together for coffee or to continue our conversation. I can't wait."

Imagine a dozen people walking away from the event with

those statements going through their heads? That's what we want! Now, on the other hand, be on the lookout for people who just might take up more of your time than can afford. That's why systems and communication rules are vital to protecting your time and funneling people into the appropriate categories (i.e., potential friend, client, moocher).

We met a very successful man named, Steve, he's a producer who would offer his time to help people in between projects. He's also a great chef. So, he offered to cook for people, to help them in various ways, someone even asked him to sponsor their book with a financial investment. It seemed there were more people who wound up taking advantage of him and didn't even offer to do anything for him in return. So, just be mindful of these situations and the kind of offers you put out there.

TAKE PICTURES & LOTS OF THEM

"Smile! Say cheese!" Don't forget to take at least one photograph of you with someone at the event. Also, take at least one photograph with you and the host of the event. After the event, you can send those photos to those you featured for their use and posting online if they choose to do so. Encourage them to do this. This is also a great time to send a thank you note to the host especially if you send your photo to them for their use as well. If they post your photo on their networking company website, just imagine the exposure you get when you do something like. It can help you with future networking events.

By taking one or more photographs at the event and posting them online, this lets others online (and those who couldn't make it to the event) know you're a mover and a shaker. Others really get the impression that you are somebody, you represent action and motivate others to want to know more about you.

Network with Bart Smith at his website → BartSmith.com

PART 2 – WHILE YOU ARE NETWORKING

In some rare, instances, be mindful about the photo you're taking and let the other person know you'd like to post it photo on your website. While it's not a requirement, it is a courtesy to ask permission. In this way, you gain instant rapport with those in the photograph. Here are the top places online you should where you could be posting your images:

Dropbox.com	TikTok	LinkedIn.com
Facebook.com	Instagram.com	PhotoBucket.com
Flickr.com	Imgur.com	Pinterest.com
FreeImage.com	Hosting.net	ImageShack.com

This is GREAT for your business and BRANDING! The more you are seen out there, even people who missed the event you attended, seeing you in so many photographs makes people feel like they already know you. This can translate easily into a call (or eMail) to you with confidence on their part. *"You just looked like someone I had to reach out to. Perhaps your services can help me. May I have a few moments of your time?"* Be sure you keep it to a few minutes to win their respect. If you need more time, ask to schedule some time with that person.

Taking photos is another great way to connect with people especially if you're taking a lot of them with groups of people. Make this a habit. Ask, *"May I have a picture taken with you?"* By the end of the night, you might end up with 10-20 good pictures. Select the best or upload all of them. Again, do send those photos to those taken in the photo so they can share them with their networks and you're on your way to becoming well known and quickly recognized while you become familiar face to many!

Network with Noa Schecter at her website → **EQevolve.com**

WALK TALL / WALK CONFIDENTLY

Walk like you are ready to pour 1,000% of energy into meeting each person (one-on-one) for the very first time ... Appear before them with a radiant smile, shoulders back, ready to lean in for a firm handshake ... even if you don't feel like you can! Practice makes perfect.

Get excited, get pumped, get into your *"happy to meet you"* mental zone so when you do meet someone new, they sense your heightened energy and feel as if they could confidently express what they do and what they need in hopes that you can help. By circulating throughout the room like this, leaving a trail of inspired conversationalists. Imagine your presence at a networking event sending out an aura of magnetic energy that attracts the right attention and reaction from people who might be saying, *"Did you meet that guy/gal? Wow, great conversation. You definitely want to meet him/her. Come with me, I'll introduce you."*

BE THE FIRST TO REACH OUT TO PEOPLE

You may not be the host of the next networking event, but there's no reason why you can't be the star by being the most accommodating person in the room reaching out to people who are struggling to meet others. While we all tend to be attracted to those people who are either the center of attention or appear successful, there are individual gems out there. All you have to do is meet them for the first time and everything else unravels nicely. So, be outgoing enough to make people feel welcomed. You might even be mistaken by some thinking that you're the host. Not a bad mistake! Accept the compliment. We never know if that quiet person may know someone who can introduce you to someone you need to meet. It's those quiet ones who can also open big doors into companies and opportunities you've been wanting to get into for a long time. Leave no stone unturned.

BE THE FIRST PERSON TO SAY, "HEY, WHAT'S YOUR NAME?"

Not initiating the *"Hello, what's your name?"* actually wastes your time. With so many people in the room to meet, you can't wait on people to come up to you. Approach them. Many people are shy and feel awkward meeting new people. Not YOU! You seize opportunities to meet new people. Take the initiative and make the first move. About 99% of the people will appreciate it. The other 1% are looking to do the same thing and meet you first. That's okay. You can take this chance to try different opening lines. Start with a compliment or ask a question about the event. *"So, have you tried anything from the buffet table yet? What looks good to you?"* Start off the conversation as if you have already been talking to them for awhile. Try different approaches besides the suggested title of this tactic. You can do better than, *"What's your name?"*

DON'T JUDGE A BOOK OR A PERSON BY ITS COVER (OR BY WHAT THE PERSON LOOKS LIKE)

This is a typical mistake people make. They think, *"Oh, look how that person is dressed or how of how he/she is not working the room. I'm not sure I want to meet that person."* Little do you know that the person you don't want to meet actually might turn out to be THE PERSON you DO want to meet! Throw away any judgmental or elitist attitudes and be open to meet anyone and everyone. Someone you haven't even met yet may be one of your biggest fans and can refer you to an ideal prospect and introduce you to a whole new world you never would have

Network with Noa Schecter at her website → **EQevolve.com**

known about had you not taken the time to disregard your prejudices and actually spend a few quality minutes talking to that person you misjudged.

BE NICE TO EVERYONE!

You never know who is standing before you, behind you or next to you. Be gracious to everyone in the room. Everyone has a story. Everyone has life's pressures, anxieties, triumphs and successes. Be generous with yourself to everyone. Again, that person you were kind to just might be the person who can help you along your journey to the next stage of your own success. People love helping others who are sincere and authentic.

TALK LESS / LISTEN MORE

Have you heard the saying? We were born with two ears and one mouth. Translated, it means don't talk too much and listen more. Let the other person do most of the talking without interrupting. This will allow you time to think about what's being said so you can reply with information and relative questions, which will make a knockout first impression. No one likes to be fire hosed to death with a non-stop spray of never ending words. Talk in sound bites and complete phrases that can be easily understood. Don't talk over someone's head and then pause in between providing ample openings for the other person to reply to what you said.

When you do talk, ask more questions versus making statements. Keep the focus on them. It's perfect to keep the conversations to about 70/30. That is, 70% represents the other person input and 30% represents your response time with valid questions to stimulate the conversation.

We have been to many networking events and listened to networkers that talked nonstop while trying to convince you that they have the best product/service since sliced bread and maybe they do. Or, maybe they're lonely and don't get out much. This is your chance to channel the conversation and make it move in the direction that gives value to both sides. Most people's brains can't remember much about a conversation, let alone all the people they met at an event. Keep conversations interesting and productive leaving an opening to continue lengthy conversations later when time permits -- possibly at another scheduled time.

If you have products/services to sell, focus on outcomes, results, and the experiences of others. Stories sell! So, there's no need to tell folks what you do if you can narrate in an entertaining and effective way. Tell stories about yourself and even better with a sense of humor. Maybe you can relate a success story that would appeal to the group and give them an idea of how you handle a certain situation. Just don't overdo it.

MAINTAIN 'A LITTLE MYSTERY' ABOUT YOURSELF WHEN TALKING TO OTHERS

Don't give away the farm and tell everyone everything about you. Retain some element of mystery about yourself encouraging people to ask you more questions. Like dating, you don't want to give everything away up front. Tease a little. Talk a little. Dance a little. Leave something to the imagination draw interest from other people. Otherwise, if you tell them everything, they might say, *"Okay, thanks for all that. I don't have any questions for you. I have to go, Maybe, we can talk later."* Don't count on it. Making people feel they want to know more for your products and services helps us to draw them closer to us. By invoking some mystique in telling your story, they're hooked. For example, many people today have few streams of income. We've been to events where people felt they needed to give you a full report on everything that was going on in their business right down to the bottom line. Focus on one topic at a time. It's not easy for people to engage in a dialogue when time is restricted. Save your other activities and interests for that important follow-up call where you will have more time to discuss various topics of mutual interest.

INTRODUCE PEOPLE TO OTHER PEOPLE

Help other people meet other people by introducing them to people you know or have just met. This is a great way for you to accelerate meeting more people provided your friends and newly made contacts at the event do the same with you. Also, in case you happen to be in charge of helping to promote an event to your friends who attend, be sure to introduce them to the host. First, you come off as a professional, and the host will appreciate the fact that you introduced your contacts to them. By doing this, you will be remembered. In the future, you've got yourself a supporter and a new friend.

This is another great reason to have your own name tag on in case the event doesn't provide them. Those people introducing you can just glance at your name tag for a quick memory check on how to introduce you. Another thing to do is to remember (and use) someone's own story when introducing them to others. "Hey (new person), I'd like you to meet _____. She just told me about _____ and I thought you should hear her story as it related to your business. (Name), tell them about what you told me regarding your success with _____."

EYE CONTACT IS IMPORTANT

Like an eagle, keep your eyes focused on the other person. You compliment the person you are listening or talking to when you look the person directly in the eye. Don't get distracted with the noise, other people's conversations that are going around you. The person standing in front of you deserves your full attention. Capture the moment and show respect for the other person talking.

PAY CLOSE ATTENTION TO OTHER PEOPLE'S BODY LANGUAGE

You can get to know someone without even talking to them by observing their body language, how they carry themselves while talking to others, their tone of voice, pitch, words they use, how well they listen, respect other speakers and so on. Pay close attention. It's those little things that can help gauge whether you want to approach someone or how much information you're willing to give up about yourself. The same observations can also help to build rapport quickly or to accelerate conversation towards a mutual means of finding common ground and moving forward with a new found business or personal relationship.

DON'T REMAIN HOSTAGE TO A DEAD-END CONVERSATION

Consider putting a time limit on how long you'll listen to someone, especially when the conversation holds no value for you. The last thing you want to do is waste your time and frequently checking your watch is not the way to go. If a person runs on and on with mundane comments, you need to take control of the conversation. You can do this without being offensive. So, here are some tips on how to ESCAPE a conversation you'd prefer not to engage in. (1) Jingle your car keys. It's a subtle psychological queue that *"It's time to go!"* (2) Excuse yourself for interrupting and say, *"Hey, let's continue this conversation after the event. I can tell you have a lot (more) to say and I'd love to hear it, but I think we should make the most*

Network with Noa Schecter at her website → **EQevolve.com**

of our time while we're both here to meet as many people as we can."

AVOID DEBATES/ ARGUMENTS & GETTING UPSET

Everyone can have their own opinion, absolutely. Just don't bring up passionate topics (or points of view) that might either lead to ruining a potential contact or your own enthusiasm for networking with the other great people. For example, when networking at a charity event, politics would not be a good topic to bring up. Stay on topic and choose to keep every conversation positive and focused on moving forward finding out how we can help each other and/or ourselves.

If someone says something you disagree with, you might reply, "I see your point. I'm glad to get another perspective on what you're talking about." You may not understand every speaker's point of view but you can respect their thoughts and ideas without compromising your own values. While politics is a hot topic these days, networking should never be the place to talk politics, religion, semantics and more. Stick to the agenda for the meeting. You'll get more out of it.

CAREFUL NOT TO OFFEND

We live in a world today where many people are hung up on political correctness, but you know the rule here: BE KIND, BE POSITIVE, BE COURTEOUS, and don't say things to people that might offend them or make them feel badly about themselves. Keep all your conversations focused on the topic at hand and make the most of what you can learn and use to your advantage. Caution: If you feel compelled to tell a joke just know that humor has its place, but it very often can backfire. If you're using it to underline a key point or message, then humor can very often let people see your human side and keep your audience's attention.

Network with Bart Smith at his website → **BartSmith.com**

It's worth mentioning to those who need to know, but avoid questions about weight, age and, "Wow, are you expecting?" Some women tend to put on weight to where they might look pregnant, but they aren't. How embarrassing for both of you. Remember the movie *Two Weeks Notice* with Hugh Grant and Sandra Bullock? There was a scene where Hugh's character congratulated a woman on being pregnant. She replied, "I'm not." Later, in the movie she was, but you get the point. DON'T ASK IF YOU DON'T KNOW.

Here's an example of what we mean when we say, watch yourself so you don't offend. We were invited to attend a networking event in Los Angeles by Noa's friend. When we showed up at the event, we almost didn't go in. We just didn't like the place we were walking into. The place turned out to be so-so, but the people proved to be fantastic! The host assured us he was looking for a new location for his next event. LESSON: After the event, instead of speaking negatively about the logistics, we actually overlooked the location and focused on the people. Had we prejudged and not gone into the event, we would never have met all those exceptional people. A week later, the host was able to find a much better location. We gained a friend and he gained two new fans for his networking organization.

DON'T COMPLAIN (OR SOUND LIKE YOU ARE)

Nobody likes to hear someone go on and on about something negative, in other words, no one likes a complainer. TIP: lead by example and never be a complainer. Don't bring up your personal laundry (or someone else's). Don't complain about an event, the food, the people, where you'd much rather be, etc. You never know when you might be offending someone who has a connection to the event. Remember what mamma said, "If you don't have anything positive to say, don't say anything at all." Zip it until you can discreetly zip out of there.

SPEAK LOUDLY & CLEARLY

This applies if you're asked to form a big circle and tell the crowd about yourself. Take a deep breath and raise your voice to a level where you can be heard by the group. When you speak, look around the room and pause to look at each person. People will appreciate and feel as if you are addressing them personally. You're also energetically connecting to them. A good thing! Remember, what kind of impression do you want to leave? If you want others to understand your message. YOU decide what and how you will make a first and lasting impression with those you meet. You want to be remembered for your entrance into the conversation and the last thing that you say to people on your way out the door. After all, you drove all the way to the event, paid your door fee to get in, and you've got a story to tell. Be proud, be loud! Well, not too loud, but be heard and clearly.

KEEP 'EM SHORT ... CONVERSATIONS, THAT IS

This kind of ties in with the MOVE ALONG / NEXT PERSON tip in Part 2, so you get the idea. Keep folks hungry for more. Let's say someone asks you a question about how you might be able to help him/her. Instead of blurting out every detail in your answer, give them just enough to pique their interest with a suggested question like, *"Let's continue this over a phone call this week, shall we?"* This is a great way for you to extend your connection to that person. *"I think I know what you're asking and I just might have the answer you are looking for. When can we talk?"*

Network with Bart Smith at his website → **BartSmith.com**

DON'T TALK ABOUT YOURSELF WITHOUT BEING ASKED, "WHAT DO YOU DO?"

It's better to wait for a queue to start talking about you, rather than to just start jump into your story with someone who: (1) doesn't care, (2) can't appreciate what you have to say/do, (3) can't use or make a positive referral for you, or (4) _____? It's better to start off any conversation focused on the other person by asking questions and learning what they do so you can figure out how best to navigate your way into talking about what you do with surgical precision.

Besides, who wants to waste time talking to someone who didn't want to know what you do anyway, only because they were so into what they do, exclusively. They had no interest in hearing what you had to say. No problem. NEXT!

IT'S OKAY TO BE VULNERABLE OR NOT KNOW SOMETHING ABOUT A PARTICULAR TOPIC

When someone is talking to you about something you don't know much about, take a virtual seat and be their student and learn. No need to fake it. Vulnerabilities attract more help and assistance than an ego maniac who thinks he/she knows it all. Just smile and say, *"Tell me more."* You can even say things like, *"I know very little about that, but I'm interested. Seriously, I'm all ears. Tell me what you know about _____."* By showing that "knowledge-seeking" side of yourself, people are encouraged to share what they know, teach, train, share, and all for FREE! It's amazing what you can learn by listening.

Network with Noa Schecter at her website → **EQevolve.com**

DOCUMENT WHAT HE/SHE/YOU SAID "IN THE MOMENT" OR "RIGHT AFTER!"

This is a biggy most people don't do and should. We all will forget a conversation or two or someone's name or what that person does. Well, no longer. If we would just commit 30 seconds (per every contact we meet) to write on a notepad or on the back of their business card, something from the conversation that we can follow up on later, then we've got it made.

Definitely carry a pen with you to the event (not everyone does) and USE IT! Create something similar to this idea to help remind you how to communicate with the person you just met. For example:

A = GREAT CONTACT   **B** = OKAY CONTACT   **C** = CYA

... or ...

BO = Business Opportunity   **CA** = Call ASAP

FR = Friend Potential   **GC** = Good Connection(s)

MI = Meet In Person   **NS** = Not Sure

Then, if you can, write down a few words or a short sentence to trigger what you two talked about. When you reconnect on the phone or in person, you know exactly where the conversation left off and where you can begin again.

MOVE ALONG ... NEXT (PERSON)

We've mentioned this already, but it's worth repeating. Don't spend too much time with any one person, unless you really believe you must. Also, don't let others spend too much time with you, either. Your job is to work the room, not have a 20-minute discussion with one stranger. Instead, five 4-minute conversations is much more fruitful for any event. Save longer conversations for follow-up calls and in-person meetings. Manage your time so energy vampires don't suck the life and time out of you. "Hey, hold that thought will you? I'll be right back ..." NO YOU WON'T!

If you go with your friends, split up, and meet other people, then your friends can introduce you to people they met and vice versa. Put yourself on your own time limit provided the event doesn't have one for the group. Give yourself 3-5 minutes TOPS. You can also go back to that person that you hoped to chat with longer, but tell them you want to work the room and agree to reconnect at another time.

The goal is to meet people, not cling to 1-3 all night long. Force yourself to say, "Let's move around and meet some other people and I'll call you this week." Then do it.

MARKET WITH EASE / BE READY TO HAND OUT YOUR MARKETING MATERIALS

Don't let your mouth do all the talking. Let your marketing materials and books do the talking for you. Don't say you wrote a book, put one in their hand so they can see it while you talk about it. Others will then see your book and join you because they're curious. By the time you explain it to the second person, the first person says, "Can I buy this?" Great, now you've created a buying domino frenzy, hopefully. Take pictures of those you just sold your book to as that will create more stir and interest in what's going on in your corner of the room.

Network with Noa Schecter at her website → **EQevolve.com**

Use a FLASH even though you don't need to. It creates a wave of interest around the room. Everyone will ask what's going on. Someone's getting photographed with an author that most will want to check out. The same goes for flyers, business cards, post cards, etc. Have them handy and ready to hand out without a flinch.

WATCH YOUR FOOD & DRINK

Do we have to mention this? If you already watch your intake, then watch out for others'. If no one drinks, the rule might be, you don't either. If others drink, be sure that you are drinking less, especially if alcohol is being served. Watch what you are eating too before/during/after the event. Check your teeth, face and clothing for food stains. Remember the purpose for being at the networking event is to NETWORK.

THANK THE HOST DURING THE EVENT
OR AT LEAST BEFORE YOU LEAVE

Never leave an event without thanking the host. If you can't do it personally, do it that night (or the next morning) via eMail, text, a comment online, etc. You might decide to leave a review on Yelp or give a testimonial on their Facebook fan page. You always want to be remembered and asked back again, personally! *"Please come back. Everyone loved meeting you!"*

SET UP YOUR FOLLOW-UP MEETINGS
WHILE YOU'RE STILL AT THE EVENT

Keep the momentum with those you meet and want to reconnect with by setting up a time/date when you two plan to talk again.

Network with Bart Smith at his website → **BartSmith.com**

Walk out of the event with at least 3 future appointments to call someone or meet them in person for coffee and then, prior to the meeting, send an eMail summarizing some of the conversation and topics you'd like to discuss when you speak next. *"It was great meeting you. I'm looking forward to continuing our conversation on _____. What else do you think we should discuss? Let me know. I look forward to our conversation."*

MAKE ONE LAST RECONNECT WITH PEOPLE PERSONALLY ON YOUR WAY OUT THE DOOR

"Hey, great meeting you. I'll call you tomorrow." Do that a few times before you leave and you'll leave a lasting impression on those people that you really want to impress so they know you are a person they would be interested in working with or brainstorming a series of ideas that would be mutually beneficial. It takes seconds to make a lasting impression, but lasts hours, days, weeks, and months on the minds of those you connected with.

MAKE ONE LAST CHECK

Did you leave anything behind? Forget anything? Take one last look around the room and check your belongings. It's hard to go back to places where people were networking and think that the coat you left behind will still be there.

PART 3

AVOID THESE NETWORKING MISTAKES

AFTER YOU GO NETWORKING

Now that the event is over and you're back home from networking, now what? Well, here are a few things to do in order to maximize your most recent networking efforts and avoid making these mistakes following your networking event. Check this out!

HOW'D YOU DO?

Evaluate how you did at the networking event. What did you learn? What did you forget to say/bring? What did you say that was good/not good. Repeat/rehearse it for next time or remember to forget it. "Whoops, I won't say/do that again." Was the event fruitful. If you're not getting what you want from the events you're attending, start looking at other events for inspiration. You should be looking at all networking events as opportunities to find ways to help others. You'd be surprised how much more effective this shift in mindset can be.

WHAT DID YOU SAY THAT ROCKED?

Yeah, what DID you say that you liked or got a glowing response. Write that down, seriously, before you forget. As you attend more networking events, continue to polish what you know will get those impressive responses. Pay attention to what you talked about that drew the most attention and got the best reactions.

WHAT DID YOU SAY THAT TANKED?

This one should be obvious! WHAT did you say to someone, about yourself, maybe something you said in response to what someone else said that was a definite no-no to use at the next event. "Yeah, I wish I could bite my tongue on that one ...", or "... take that one back!" Hopefully you didn't say something you need to apologize for because if you do, then don't ignore this faux pas. A sincere apology may be in order.

CREATE YOUR OWN SYSTEM FOR ORGANIZING THE LEADS YOU GOT FROM THE NETWORKING EVENT

The biggest mistake people make after networking is failing to use a CRM (Customer Relationship Management) system to capture momentum before it fades. Without a structured way to log names, the specific event where you met, and detailed notes on what you discussed, valuable conversations are forgotten and business cards simply gather dust.

To turn a brief encounter into a long-term connection, you must take immediate action by scanning cards and categorizing leads into a simple priority system: (1) Urgent Call, (2) Warm Follow-up or (3) General/Unsure. By documenting specific talking points while they are fresh, you can follow up the next day with precision, proving you were truly listening and establishing yourself as a professional who follows through.

However, the "best" CRM isn't the most popular or the fanciest one—it is the one that fits your company's size, sales process, and team habits. A solo entrepreneur may prioritize the simplicity of HubSpot or the all-in-one marketing tools of GoHighLevel.com, while larger organizations may require the deep customization of Zoho or Salesforce. Choosing a system just because someone else loves it is a recipe for an expensive, unused tool. The real secret to success is selecting a platform that aligns with how you actually work, ensuring that it becomes a consistent part of your daily routine rather than a frustrating digital hurdle.

Network with Bart Smith at his website → BartSmith.com

SHARE YOUR NEWLY FORMED CONTACTS WITH YOUR CURRENT FRIENDS/COLLEAGUES

Not many people ever think of sharing their networking experience with their friends and colleagues who didn't attend the event. It's always courteous (not a requirement) to ask permission from those you met to share their information with your inner circle of friends, associates, and colleagues. Even if it's a phone number or eMail, ask permission first. Once you get their okay, reach out to make introductions in a timely manner, not weeks from the day you met the person.

OUT OF SIGHT, OUT OF MIND (FOLLOW-UP IS ESSENTIAL)

About 99% of people who say they're interested in following up with you ... never do! So, YOU take the initiative, do the grown-up thing, and follow up because 99% of the time, the person you're reaching out to will appreciate that you took the first step.

It usually takes 2-3 more communications for that new contact to become a new friend/contact. So, keep the momentum going after the event when people still remember who you are. If you wait too long, and you feel the other person has some hesitation in reaching out to you, again, you take that next step and make the call. Don't let your own networking efforts go to waste and you reach out to them.

If you take notes on business cards or paper or in your phone about your conversations, it'll be easy to call people in order to pick up from where you left off. Use the notes in order to create a personal message via eMail or voice mail if you don't reach them. They'll be impressed.

Some folks are great at getting back to people. They call people every 6 months or send them handwritten cards for holidays and birthdays. Again, people are impressed with follow ups and eventually will give them their business if there's a match.

MAXIMIZE & CAPITALIZE

So, you got some fresh leads from the event you just attended. Jump on them, follow-up promptly, and see them through to the end to where you turn those leads into sales! Create your own follow-up chart, especially if you met a number of people you want to follow-up with. Work your chart by calling people, leaving notes next to their name, such as LM (Left Message) or CB (Call Back) or WCM (Will Call Me).

If you happen to call their home or office and speak to someone other than the person you're calling, be respectful. Qualify what you are calling about and how much you are looking forward to talking with the new contact that you made. You never know what the relationship is. You definitely want to hear a nice report about how you handled your call with them. "Yes, that was my wife that you spoke to. She really enjoyed the brief conversation you had about our products."

POST YOUR NETWORKING RESULTS ON YOUR WEBSITE & SOCIAL MEDIA ACCOUNTS

Post your networking results on all of your social media accounts after every event. Do the rounds; post what you did, where you went, who you met (i.e., give 3-5 people a plug/mention), thank the host, talk about something you learned, etc. Help promote people you met offline and online!

Pick out 3-5 people you thought were most interesting and mention their website or other online presence so people in your inner circle can learn more about them. Say, "Hello" to those you met in social media. LIKE their Facebook fan page, post a comment, upload a photo, tag yourself in a photo, etc.

START PREPARING FOR THE NEXT NETWORKING OPPORTUNITY

To make the next networking event even more successful, start preparing for it now. Order more books or supplies if you need to. No doubt, if you brought books or product for sale, you might need to order more to replenish what you sold. Keep your eye on the calendar for shipping reasons. The next networking event might be coming up soon. Get a jump on orders and shipping times. Maybe you need to get new copies of what you handed out. Same thing. Jump on it now while it's fresh on your mind, and not the night before the next event. Bring cash for change. If you didn't have a credit card swiper or app for your phone to accept credit cards, don't show up to the next event without one. Order it today! Whatever else you think you might need, order it, now. Don't be caught off guard going to the next event.

NETWORK YOUR WAY & HOST YOUR OWN NETWORKING EVENTS

Do you think you can do a better job at hosting your own networking event? Would your business benefit more if you

Network with Noa Schecter at her website → **EQevolve.com**

conducted your own meet and greet event with friends and clients in your industry of expertise? Then, by all means, start the groundwork to create your own events or MeetUp group, especially if you're new in your area.

What have you learned from the networking events you've attended? What can you improve on? What would you gain by having your own event? It's so easy to conduct your own events these days with MeetUp.com and Zoom.com. You don't even have to leave your home. You can create groups online and network with others around the country.

Whether you're networking to socialize or to promote a book, product or service in today's world, it's so easy to start your own networking event. MeetUp.com provides all the tools! Decide on a topic for your event and look forward to networking with others who share your interests.

Join a few other MeetUp groups for creative ideas on how to start your own group before you actually take the plunge. You can eventually alternate between your events and other groups to bring even more people together. In the beginning, like everything else, it may take time to build. Be persistent and go to few others to learn how to make yours a total success.

■ ■ ■

BONUS SECTION
10 SOCIAL MEDIA NETWORKING MISTAKES

"Visibility may open the door, but trust is what keeps it open." — Noa Schecter

"Social networking isn't about collecting a digital crowd; it's about planting a digital garden where every genuine seed of conversation grows into a forest of shared opportunity." — Bart Smith

Social media has changed the way we meet people, stay visible, and create opportunities. A single post, a thoughtful comment, or a well-timed message can open the door to a new relationship, a collaboration, or even a life-changing business connection.

But let's not confuse access with connection. Social media helps people notice you, but it does not build the relationship for you. Too many people chase attention instead of trust; they focus on being seen but forget how to make people feel something real.

Used wisely, social media strengthens your network. Used poorly, it can quietly weaken your credibility and push the right people away. If you want your online presence to support your networking instead of sabotaging it, avoid these mistakes.

10 SOCIAL MEDIA NETWORKING MISTAKES

MISTAKE #1
Using Social Media to Broadcast Instead of Connect

One of the most common mistakes people make is treating social media like a billboard. Every post is about what they are selling, promoting, or launching; but while the content may be polished, if everything feels like a one-way announcement, people eventually feel disconnected.

Networking is not built through announcements; it is built through conversation, shared value, and the feeling that there is a real person behind the profile. People do not want to feel marketed to all day long.

Network with Noa Schecter at her website → **EQevolve.com**

Instead, they crave authenticity and relevance. They want to feel there is a genuine relationship available not just another pitch waiting for them.

MISTAKE #2
Wanting Engagement Without Giving It

Many people want to be seen, but few are actually willing to participate. They scroll, post, and watch, hoping others will notice them while rarely taking the time to comment thoughtfully, support someone else's success, or contribute to a conversation. This is not networking; it is simply spectating.

Real networking on social media begins in small moments a genuine comment, a thoughtful reply, a shared post, or a simple acknowledgement that says, "I see you." These interactions transform passive observation into active connection.

Ultimately, people remember who made them feel noticed and who showed up with generosity. By shifting from spectating to contributing, you build a reputation rooted in support and meaningful engagement.

MISTAKE #3
Leading With A Pitch Instead Of A Relationship

Very little turns people off faster than a direct message that feels like a sales script. You accept a connection request, and moments later, a polished, strategic message arrives that immediately makes you feel like a target instead of a person. While there is nothing wrong with doing business through social media, trust has no room to grow when the first interaction feels purely transactional. The best networkers understand that timing is everything. They know that connection must come before conversion and that rapport always precedes a request. By leading with curiosity rather than pressure, they open doors that a cold pitch never could.

MISTAKE #4
Collecting Connections Instead Of Building Them

Some people treat social media like a numbers game—chasing more followers, more connections, and more names in the feed. Yet, for all this activity, very little relationship-building actually happens. They connect with people only to disappear, offering no follow-up, no continued interaction, and no effort to deepen the connection. This becomes the digital version of collecting business cards only to toss them into a drawer.

A connection is not a relationship; it is only an introduction. The real value begins after the connection is made—when you engage, follow up, and stay visible in a meaningful way. By allowing trust to build over time, you transform a simple digital contact into a valuable partnership.

MISTAKE #5
Having an Online Presence That Weakens Your Credibility

Before someone responds to your message or accepts a request, they will do something very simple: they will look at your profile. In seconds, they will form an impression based on your photo, bio, headline, recent posts, and overall energy.

If your profile is incomplete, unclear, outdated, or inconsistent with your professional image, you may lose credibility before

Network with Noa Schecter at her website → **EQevolve.com**

the conversation even starts. Your profile does not need to be perfect, but it does need to feel intentional. It should quickly communicate who you are, what you do, and the kind of presence people can expect from you. By presenting a clear and cohesive digital identity, you ensure that your first impression supports the relationships you are trying to build.

MISTAKE #6
Posting Without Clarity, Consistency Or Purpose

Some people post constantly for a week, only to disappear for six weeks, eventually returning with content that feels random, reactive, or disconnected from their professional identity. This inconsistency creates confusion; if people cannot tell what you care about, what you stand for, or the value you bring, they will struggle to remember you clearly. In networking, clarity matters.

You do not need to post every day or become a content machine, but if you want social media to support your networking, your presence must feel intentional. Your content should reinforce your identity, reflecting your values, your expertise, your energy, and your voice.

MISTAKE #7
Turning Every Interaction Back to Yourself

This mistake is subtle, but people feel it immediately. Someone shares a success and, instead of celebrating them, you turn the moment back to your own story; someone posts a challenge and, within seconds, the conversation turns to your opinion, expertise, or service. While it may not always be intentional, it is highly noticeable. The strongest networkers know how to

Network with Bart Smith at his website → **BartSmith.com**

make other people feel important. They understand how to listen, stay curious, and ask questions that deepen the connection rather than redirecting the attention to themselves. This is true in person, and it is just as true online.

MISTAKE #8
Treating Every New Contact Like a Potential Sale

This is one of the fastest ways to damage trust on social media. Not every person who enters your world is supposed to become a customer, and not every interaction needs to be a business opportunity. When you view every new connection through the lens of "What can I sell here?" people feel that energy immediately. When someone senses an agenda rather than genuine interest, they naturally pull back, and what could have been a meaningful relationship begins to feel like a transaction.

Great networking is rarely built by forcing outcomes too early. Sometimes the right person becomes a client, a referral source, or a collaborator. Other times, they simply become a valuable relationship that opens a door years later. By focusing on the person rather than the pitch, you allow these diverse opportunities to develop naturally over time.

MISTAKE #9
Forgetting That Your Online Behavior Is Part of Your Reputation

Social media gives people a front-row seat to how you show up—not just in what you say, but how you say it. Your audience is watching how you respond, how you disagree, and how you handle both attention and tension. This is where many people quietly hurt their networking; public arguments, reactive

Network with Noa Schecter at her website → **EQevolve.com**

comments, over-tagging, or using cold automation all communicate a specific message about your character. While your content tells people what you know, your behavior tells them what it might feel like to work with you. Chasing visibility with forced, performative, or overly polarizing behavior can quickly undermine your credibility. Professionalism does not mean being bland, but it does mean being grounded in how you engage with others online.

MISTAKE #10
Forgetting That Social Media Is Only the Beginning

This may be the most important reminder of all: social media matters, and it can absolutely help you build visibility, stay relevant, and create opportunities. It introduces you to people you may never have met otherwise and starts conversations that lead to extraordinary things. However, social media is still only the beginning. A like is not a relationship, a follower is not trust, a comment is not a connection, and visibility alone is not influence.

The strongest relationships are still built the same way they have always been: through real conversation, presence, emotional intelligence, shared energy, consistency, and genuine care. A post may open the door and a message may begin the conversation, but the real relationship begins when you take it one step further. Whether it is a one-on-one conversation, a phone call, a Zoom meeting, or a coffee, these are the moments where someone can truly experience who you are. The real work happens in the thoughtful follow-up and the transition from the public feed to a private, personal connection.

■ ■ ■

Network with Bart Smith at his website → BartSmith.com

CONCLUSION
LET'S SUM IT UP

CONCLUSION – LET'S SUM IT UP

Mistakes happen. Can we correct them? You bet. Will we repeat them? Maybe a few, from time to time. Who's perfect? Your networking success can be based 100% on what you do before, during, and after every networking event. Now that you know this to be true, what are you going to do to make your networking efforts more productive and prosperous?

Here's a list of the **TOP 15 THINGS** we developed based on our experiences in order to "sum it up" what we've learned about networking! Take control, take action, and win every time you go networking!

1. Make a list of things you need to do before each event.

2. Prepare yourself personally & emotionally for the event.

3. Prepare any marketing materials and supplies you need to take to the event.

4. What will be your outcome/goal for attending the event?

5. Keep conversations short enough to be able to move around the room to meet other people.

6. Ask more questions. Get the other person to talk more about themselves and not so much about you.

7. Make notes on cards or paper about the conversations you're having with those at the event so you don't forget.

8. Thank the host during the event.

9. Set up 1-3 appointments during the event in order to contact those individuals after the event.

10. Say goodbye one last time to those you meet at the event as you walk out the door to go home.

Network with Noa Schecter at her website → **EQevolve.com**

11. What did you learn from the event? The good, the bad and the ugly? What rocked? What tanked?

12. Follow-up quickly after the event with your new contacts via text, eMail, phone or both. Remember, 99% of those you met won't. So, YOU take the first step to reconnect. They'll appreciate it.

13. Post some of the photos you took and mention their names and websites on your social media accounts and/or website.

14. Prepare for the next event coming up.

15. Start your own events!

That's it! How'd you do? What do you think? Think this list (and this book) will help turn you into a networking rock star? We'd like to know. Contact us at our website and tell us your networking story. Let us hear from you! In the meantime, keep on networking armed with useful information and proven experiences. Life and success is a people business. Networking is one of the main ingredients that helps us all get there.

To your "networking" success,

BART SMITH
BartSmith.com
LinkedIn.com/in/BartSmith

NOA SCHECTER
EQEvolve.com
LinkedIn.com/in/NoaSchecter

NOTES NOTES NOTES

After reading *51+ NETWORKING MISTAKES*, what stood out for you? What kinds of mistakes do you want to avoid the next time you go out networking? What do you want to say/do/bring the next time you go networking? Take a few moments to reflect and jot down a few notes about that. Then, make it happen!

www.ingramcontent.com/pod-product-compliance
Lightning Source LLC
Chambersburg PA
CBHW071823200526
45169CB00018B/922